LIVING BY FAITH THROUGH THE MIDLIFE YEARS

Forty Devotions to Empower You for the Journey

JEANINNE STOKES

First paperback edition April 2024

Book Cover design by Lakisha Walton

ISBN 979-8-218-39440-0 (paperback)

ISBN 9798218398453 (eBook)

Published by JStokes Publishing Company

CONTENTS

INTRODUCTION

Your family relationships are changing. You're walking the tightrope, balancing your career and home. You're launching children out of the nest and caring for aging parents while worrying if you're saving enough for your retirement years. You're not in the Twilight Zone. You're in your midlife years.

What are the midlife years? According to Psychologytoday.com, midlife is generally acknowledged as the years between one's early 40s to early 60s, but there's about 10 years of wiggle room on either side of this range. These years can be one of the most taxing seasons of a woman's life as she deals with the multiple stressors that can occur. Stressors may include work/life balance, changing family dynamics, aging parents, financial challenges, becoming an empty nester, health challenges, and the biggie—menopause. These stressors can test the faith of any woman, causing her to wonder if she'll ever make it to a peaceful existence again.

The author has journeyed through these years, has had her faith tested and her spirit anchored, and has written this pocketbook of devotions to offer a source of ongoing encouragement for women as they navigate their midlife years. By sharing uplifting and affirming thoughts from scripture that address the various challenges midlife presents, she points women to the God who can help them survive their midlife years and come out triumphantly on the other side.

So whether you're sipping your morning coffee before another hectic day of work or sneaking a moment of solace from a house full of noisy grandchildren, dip into these devotions. For in this sacred space you will discover that midlife isn't a twilight zone—it's a place where faith can bloom anew.

WHEN YOU'RE

WAITING FOR
AN ANSWER

HE'S STILL WORKING

Wait for the Lord; be strong and take heart
and wait for the Lord.
Psalms 27:14 NIV

Nothing irks me more as I live my midlife years than arriving on time at my doctor's office and then waiting for what seems like an eternity until the nurse tells me the doctor is ready to see me. I did my part. I scheduled my appointment. I arrived on time. It doesn't seem fair that I must sit…and wait.

But when I finally saw my doctor and he explained the reason for the wait, I was not upset anymore because I learned there was a purpose for the wait.

Oftentimes, I also get upset at my heavenly Father when it seems like it is taking Him a while to answer my prayers. Why is it taking so long for Him to answer my prayer for healing from a health issue I've battled for years? Why is it taking so long for Him to answer my prayer for my mother who can't seem to remember who I am anymore? Or my prayer for my young adult child battling an addiction they can't seem to overcome?

When we find ourselves wondering why it seems to be taking so long for God to respond to our prayers as we live our midlife years, we can find solace in knowing that God is actively working behind the scenes of our lives, working to answer our prayers in His own time and way.

That's what I believe pastor and author Max Lucado meant when he wrote the following words: "God is always at work. He never twiddles his thumbs. He takes no vacations. God is always working because He is an active God."[1]

Like my doctor who was actively working behind the scenes to ensure my visit would be successful, be encouraged knowing that while waiting for an answer to your prayers, God is working. Actively working out His best plans for you as you live your midlife years.

PRAY

Father, help me to trust You today
that while I am waiting for an answer
to my prayers as I live my midlife
years, You are actively working
behind the scenes for my good.
Amen.

DIGGING DEEPER

In what ways are you in the waiting
room of prayer right now as you live
your midlife years? What do you
believe God wants you to learn about
Him while there?

*I waited patiently for the Lord to help me,
and he turned to me and heard my cry.*
Psalms 40:1

CLIMB ON UP

*I will climb up to my watchtower and stand
at my guard post. There I will wait to see
what the Lord says and how He will
answer my complaint.*
Habakkuk 2:1

During biblical times, watchtowers were built on city walls. It was a position a watchman took to patiently watch and wait to let his city know if any enemies or messengers were approaching.

Habakkuk the prophet shared his concerns with God about the myriad of problems that were occurring in his homeland, including their probable imminent destruction at the hands of the powerful Babylonian army. He told God that like a watchman on the city walls, he would climb up and expectantly wait for God to respond to his concerns. His climbing into his "watchtower" was a beautiful illustration of his belief that God had not only heard his concern but would eventually answer.

What are some pressing concerns you have as you live your midlife years? Are you asking: Why is my good health failing? Why am I going through so much drama at my job? Why do I keep having marital problems when I have been a loyal wife?

When your mind and heart are riddled with questions as you live your midlife years, present your concerns to your heavenly Father, for He is a God who can handle every question you pose to Him. Then like a watchman on the city walls, climb up into your "watchtower" and expectantly wait for Him to answer.

PRAY

Father, thank You for hearing my concerns today as I live my midlife years. I trust You to answer my prayers in Your own time and way. Amen.

DIGGING DEEPER

What specific questions do you have for God as you live your midlife years?
How will you wait with a sense of expectation that He will answer your prayers?

Wait patiently for the Lord. Be brave and courageous. Yes, wait patiently for the Lord.
Psalms 27:14

WHEN THE ANSWER IS NO

And we know that God causes everything
to work together for the good of those who
love God and are called according to his
purpose for them.
Romans 8:28

"Father, I ask for healing for my friend's husband as he lies again in a hospital bed. You've healed him before, heavenly Father. Please heal him again."

This was the prayer I prayed with my friend early one morning after receiving a call that her husband had been hospitalized. But after praying with her for God to heal her husband, she called later to tell me he died.

Why does God say no to our earnest prayers as we live our midlife years? Our prayers for healing from sickness for ourselves or our loved ones. Our prayers for the restoration of the health of our frail and aging parents. Our prayers for the healing of a broken marriage.

The apostle Paul's life offers insight as to why God may say no to our prayers. While serving as a missionary and preacher to the Gentiles, he asked God to heal him three times from a "thorn in his flesh". Each time God said no. Not because He did not love His great servant or empathize with Paul's health problem, but because He wanted to use Paul's problem to help him focus on his constant dependence on Him.

What are you earnestly praying for today as you live your midlife years? A less stressful job? Healing from a recurring health problem? That God would heal your marriage or spouse who is battling cancer? The possibilities are endless for the things we need and desire as we live our midlife years, but what do you do when you earnestly submit a request to the Lord and the answer returns no?

Keep trusting that His grace is sufficient through it all.

PRAY

Father, it hurts when You say no to
my prayers, but help me to
keep believing as I live my midlife
years that You know what is best for
me. Amen.

DIGGING DEEPER

Has God said no to a prayer request
as you live your midlife years? Why
do you think He is saying no to your
request?

*Furthermore, because we are united with
Christ, we have received an inheritance from
God, for he chose us in advance, and he
makes everything work out according to his
plan.*
Ephesians 1:11

KEEP ROOTING FOR
THE HOME TEAM

*It is good that a man should both hope and
quietly wait for the salvation of the Lord.
Lamentations 3:26 KJV*

When my city's professional team is in a difficult season, fans are quick to say they don't know if the team's problems can be fixed. After all, no one sees any signs from the games they've played that indicate they will get any better. They simply have no faith that their professional football team can overcome their problems and become an effective team again. They have forgotten their team is part of a great organization that has overcome before when faced with adversity.

Have you also lost hope in your home team as you live your midlife years? Your team of the Father, Son, and Holy Spirit? Perhaps you're facing recurring debt, a difficult relationship with a rebellious child, or a demanding job. You've lost hope because you don't see any signs that the problem in your life is going to get any better.

The Word of God reminds us that it is good to hope and quietly wait for the salvation of the Lord. What that means is when we find ourselves ready to give up when problems occur that we can't seem to overcome, we are to keep believing that a change will eventually arrive. Why? Because we have a wonderful team comprised of the Father, Son, and Holy Spirit, and experience has shown us if we hang in there, our "teammates" will help us win at life again.

So don't give up hope on your home team as you live your midlife years. Keep rooting for them.

PRAY

Father, as I wait for You to answer my prayers as I live my midlife years, may I never lose hope in my home team. Amen.

DIGGING DEEPER

How have you given up hope because of a difficult problem that is occurring now that you are in your midlife years? What do you need to do to renew your faith in the home team of the Father, Son, and Holy Spirit?

Rejoice in our confident hope. Be patient in trouble and keep on praying.
Romans 12:12

WHEN YOU'RE

FIGHTING A
BATTLE

FIGHTING WITH THE RIGHT WEAPONS

The weapons we fight with are not the weapons of the world. On the contrary, they have divine power to demolish strongholds.
II Corinthians 10:4 NIV

Do you remember the blockbuster movie *The War Room*? It tells the story of a disillusioned wife who kept fighting for her marriage to survive. But due to the disinterest of her husband to save it, it appeared she would lose the battle until a chance meeting occurred between her and an older Christian woman. After listening to the older woman's counsel about the weapons to use to fight for the marriage and implementing her suggestions, restoration occurred in the young woman's marriage.

Like the young married woman seeking to save her marriage, we cannot fight our great enemy—the devil—using our methods when he seeks to destroy our lives. His attacks will be too strong for us to overcome on our own. Instead, the apostle Paul encourages us to use an arsenal of mighty weapons to fight against the devil's attacks on our lives. The weapons include the "belt of truth" to fight against the lies he tells us that sound like truth; the "body armor of righteousness" to protect our hearts from becoming discouraged; the "shoes of peace" to help us continue walking in His peace when we are overcome with worry; the "sword of the Spirit" that helps us fight by recalling and reciting what the Bible says about our lives; the "shield of faith" to help us combat every piercing arrow that seeks to penetrate our heart to destroy our belief in God's promises; and the "helmet of salvation" which keeps us from doubting who we are and the security we have in Him. (Ephesians 6:10-18)

Are you under attack like never before as you live your midlife years? Don't try to fight using your weapons. Fight using His.

PRAY

Father, thank You that I can win the
attacks the great enemy aims at me
by using Your mighty weapons.
Amen.

DIGGING DEEPER

Read Ephesians 6:10-18, then make a
list of the spiritual weapons you will
use to fight your battles as you live
your midlife years.

*Stay alert! Watch out for your great enemy,
the Devil. He prowls around like a roaring
lion, looking for someone to devour.*
I Peter 5:8

WATCHING WHAT YOU EAT

So I say, let the Holy Spirit guide your
lives. Then you won't be doing what your
sinful nature craves.
Galatians 5:16

I have had a thin frame most of my life, but as I age, I am picking up weight in areas of my body I never expected. However, my doctor reminded me at my last checkup that I don't have to lose my battle of weight gain as I grow older if I pay attention to what I'm feeding myself.

Similarly, we don't have to lose the great spiritual shape we have acquired through the years as Christian women now that we are living our midlife years if we are watching what we feed ourselves. Like the daily choice we must make about what to eat to prevent our bodies from gaining weight, every day we must also choose which foods we'll eat to help us stay in great spiritual shape. Will we feed on the "foods" that produce the fruit of love, joy, peace, patience, kindness, goodness, faithfulness, gentleness, and self-control? Or will we feed on those "foods" that produce the fruit of hostility, quarreling, jealousy, outbursts of anger, selfishness, and division? (See Galatians 5:19-23)

The battle of maintaining both your physical and spiritual shape is a battle you will face every day as you live your midlife years. But like my doctor told me, it's a battle you can win if you watch what you eat.

PRAY

Father, grant me the desire to feed on the right "foods" as I live my midlife years to help me stay in great spiritual shape. Amen.

DIGGING DEEPER

How is your spiritual diet looking today? What can you do to ensure you are eating the right foods?

Since we are living by the Spirit, let us follow the Spirit's leading in every part of our lives.
Galatians 5:25

DRESSING FOR SUCCESS

*Put on the full armor of God, so that you
can take your stand against the devil's
schemes.*
Ephesians 6:11 NIV

When I began my career, I attended a class that taught me how to dress for success as a young professional. I remember how helpful this class was, for it taught me the color of clothes that were right for my skin tone, what type of clothes to purchase to fit my body type, and the appropriate shoes to wear as a professional woman. After attending the class, I came away confident I was ready to dress for success.

In his letter to the Ephesians believers, the apostle Paul reminded them of the importance of also dressing for success. Because there was a spiritual war going on between the forces of good and evil in the world, there were certain clothes Paul recommended they wear to help them win the battle. Clothes that are included in Ephesians 6:

- The belt of truth (v. 14)

- The body armor of righteousness (v. 14)

- The shoes of peace (v. 15)

- The shield of faith (v. 16)

- The helmet of salvation (v. 17)

- The sword of the spirit (v. 17)

There's still a war going on between the forces of good and evil as you live your midlife years. But there's no need to worry, for as long as you dress for success, you can win!

PRAY

Father, thank You for the clothes
You have provided to help me dress
for success as I live my midlife years.
Amen.

DIGGING DEEPER

Which item(s) in your spiritual closet
do you need to put on today to help
you dress for success as you live your
midlife years?

*Above all, clothe yourselves with love, which
binds us all together in perfect harmony.*
Colossians 3:14

USING YOUR SIMPLE EQUIPMENT

When David prepared to fight the giant Goliath, King Saul told David to wear his armor. But after David took a couple of steps, he told the king he could not wear his armor because he wasn't used to wearing it. Instead, David used what he was comfortable with to fight wild animals while protecting his sheep—his shepherd's staff, his slingshot, and some stones.

Oftentimes, we think we need extraordinary materials to slay the giants we encounter in our lives as we live our midlife years; giants like when your young adult child tells you he no longer believes in God and wants to live a lifestyle that contradicts your Christian beliefs; giants like when your doctor gives you riveting news that you have a rare form of cancer; giants like when your spouse tells you he doesn't love you anymore and wants a divorce.

But David's battle with the giant Goliath demonstrates that God uses simple, ordinary materials to help us deal with our great problems. A small stone, for example, helps David defeat Goliath; a staff helps Moses deliver the Israelites from Egypt; a horn helps Joshua flatten the walls of Jericho.

What are the simple, ordinary materials God has given you to fight the giant you face in your life today as you live your midlife years? Unyielding faith and trust in Him? A powerful prayer life? Standing strong on the promises found in the Holy Word? Don't negate the equipment God has given you to fight your great battles. For with it He can do through you extraordinary things.

PRAY

Father, thank You for the simple equipment You have given me from Your Holy Word to conquer my life giants. Amen.

DIGGING DEEPER

What type of giant do you face today in your life as a midlife woman? How will you use the simple equipment of prayer, faith, and God's promises to help you conquer your giant?

A final word: Be strong in the Lord and in his mighty power.
Ephesians 6:10

WHEN YOUR

FAITH IS BEING
CHALLENGED

TAP INTO YOUR POWER

But you will receive power when the Holy Spirit comes upon you. And you will be my witnesses, telling people about me everywhere—in Jerusalem, throughout Judea, in Samaria, and to the ends of the earth.
Acts 1:8

No matter how well a pyrotechnician creates a spectacular firework to be displayed on the canvas of a night sky, it will never display without one main feature—dynamite. The dynamite provides the power that causes the firework to showcase its beauty across the canvas of the night sky.

Just like a firework cannot be displayed without the power of dynamite, we cannot live our lives effectively during our midlife years without the dynamic power of the Holy Spirit. Jesus made this clear when He told His disciples they would need to use the power of the Holy Spirit after He ascended to heaven. That power would be necessary for them to continue doing the work of evangelism that He commissioned them to do. Paul made it clear when he told Timothy he would need to use the power that resided within him to overcome his fear and timidity as a young pastor. This is the same power Jesus used when He healed the woman with the issue of blood.

Can I run a marathon I've always wanted to run? Can I overcome my fear of flying and take a trip to a destination I've always wanted to visit? Can I go back to school to finish my degree now that I am an empty nester?

When you doubt your ability to recreate a new life for yourself as you live your midlife years, remember to tap into your power—the dynamic power of the Holy Spirit that resides within you to live life magnificently.

PRAY

Father, thank You for the dynamic power of the Holy Spirit that allows me to live life magnificently for You during my midlife years. Amen.

DIGGING DEEPER

What is the life you seek to create as you live your midlife years?
How will you tap into the Spirit's power within
to create the life you desire?

Now all glory to God, who is able, through his mighty power at work within us, to accomplish infinitely more than we might ask or think.
Ephesians 3:20

DON'T THROW IT AWAY

*So do not throw away this confident trust in
the Lord. Remember the great reward it
brings you.*
Hebrews 10:35

"You will be okay once you've healed and gone back to teaching your children again at church."

"I'm not going back. I'm done with church and with God."

Those were the words a young woman told her mother after awakening from surgery and learning she would not be able to have children. The news was even more devastating to hear because just before the surgery, she had accepted a marriage proposal from her long-time boyfriend. Although she had been known for her strong faith, after hearing of her infertility, she tore her treasured cross from her neck and denounced her faith in God.

There is no escaping it. Everyone who desires to live the Christian life will experience suffering (II Timothy 3:12). This suffering includes that which you will experience as you live through your midlife years. Your department on your job went through a major reorganization, and your company released you just when you were about to retire. You lost both parents within months and you're now trying to figure out how to live life without them. You desperately need a medical procedure to improve your overall health, yet your insurance company keeps denying coverage.

How do you continue living life during your midlife years when at times, the sufferings you experience become too much for you to bear?

Keep your eyes on the One who endured. Jesus Christ was ridiculed when He shared His message with the Jews, yet He endured. He was misunderstood by His family, yet He endured. He was beaten, spit on, and taunted by the Roman soldiers as He walked the road to Calvary, yet He endured. And He endured as He hung and died on an old, rugged cross. Because Jesus endured, as He prepares for His return, He now sits at the place of highest honor next to His Father in heaven.

Are you ready to cast away your faith as you live your midlife years? Keep looking to the One who endured.

PRAY

Father, when the sufferings I experience are more than I feel I can manage as I live my midlife years, remind me to keep looking to the One who endured. Amen.

DIGGING DEEPER

In what ways are you ready to cast away your faith in God as you live your midlife years? What can you do today to convince yourself to keep holding on?

We can rejoice, too, when we run into problems and trials, for we know that they help us develop endurance
Romans 5:3

TWENTY-FOUR, SEVEN

I have told you all this so you may have peace in me. Here on earth you will have many trials and sorrows. But take heart because I have overcome the world.
John 16:33

A preacher told a story one Sunday about a football player who blamed God because he dropped an easy game-winning touchdown that would have allowed his team to win the game leading them to the Superbowl. Later that evening in his hotel room, he tweeted his frustrations to God: *I praise You 24/7, and this is how You do me. I'll never forget this! Ever!*

Have you ever voiced these same words to God? Have you ever been angry at Him because you sought to live your life faithfully during your midlife years, yet He still allowed you to lose your house? Your job? Your health?

God never promised life would be perfect as we live our midlife years. The feeling of throwing in the proverbial towel on living a life of faith is nothing more than a challenge from the enemy of our souls. Don't fall for it. Keep believing that our heavenly Father knows best and is working out His plan for our overall good. His plans are designed to help us look more and more like Him.

An abrupt ending to your career. A strained and distant relationship between you and a sibling. The loss of your treasured home after falling behind on your property taxes. Life's difficulties may cause you to say, "God, is this how you do me as I live my midlife years?"

But hear God answering, "Yes, dear child, but I hope you'll decide to keep serving Me anyway. Twenty-four-seven."

PRAY

Father, no matter what happens in
my life as I live my midlife years, may
it never cause me to stop loving and
serving You – twenty-four, seven.
Amen.

DIGGING DEEPER

What is happening in your life as you
live your midlife years that is causing
you to feel God has let you down? In
what ways will you keep serving God
anyway, despite your
disappointment?

*For God has said, "I will never fail you
I will never abandon you."*
Hebrews 13:5(b)

DON'T FORGET

And whatever you do or say, do it as a
representative of the Lord Jesus, giving
thanks through him to God the Father.
Colossians 3:17

Occasionally I hear athletes say they should not have to be examples for others, especially when they are not representing their teams on the playing field. However, the athlete fails to realize that whether they are in uniform or not, they are still representatives.

Similarly, those of us who have chosen to wear the name of Jesus Christ can't just represent Him when it's convenient to do so, for the Bible tells us that we are to always represent Jesus Christ. Whether we're standing in a long line at the grocery store that is trying our last bit of patience after a long day's work, arguing with our spouse over who's supposed to cook dinner, fussing at our children about a poor decision they have made, or losing our patience with an elderly parent, we are called to represent Christ as we deal with the various challenges of our midlife years in everything we say and do.

So during those moments when you're tempted to forget who you are as you live your midlife years, remember…you are a representative.

PRAYER

Father, wherever I go and whatever I do as I live my midlife years, may I never forget who I represent. Amen.

DIGGING DEEPER

In what ways have you forgotten who you represent as you live your midlife years? How will you become a better representative today?

So whether you eat or drink, or whatever you do, do it all for the glory of God.
I Corinthians 10:31

WHEN YOU

NEED COMFORT

LOOK TO THE LIGHT

Praise be to the God and Father of our Lord
Jesus Christ, the Father of compassion and
the God of all comfort.
II Corinthians 1:3 NIV

As a young boy, while sitting on the porch of his home outside of the city, my uncle shared how he could see the city lights over the horizon. When his mother became ill and was taken away, he would periodically ask his caregiver where his mother was and she would reply, "Look to the lights, for your mother is somewhere within the lights."

In the same way my uncle received comfort during his mother's illness by looking towards the city lights, we have a source we can look to for comfort when we need it the most as we live our midlife years. For the Bible declares that God is the source of every type of comfort. Comfort when you have laid both parents to rest and are learning to live life without them; comfort when your children have all left the nest and you're all alone in an empty home; comfort when you receive a riveting health diagnosis; comfort when you've signed the papers for your marriage to end.

Are you in need of comfort today as you live your midlife years? Look to the heavenly lights, for God is right there, waiting to wrap his arms around you and provide you with the comfort that only He can give.

PRAY

Father, thank You for being the
ultimate source of comfort for me as
I live my midlife years. Amen.

DIGGING DEEPER

Make a list of the scripture verses
that provide a special source of
comfort to you during challenging
times, then post your list in a
conspicuous place to remind you of
God's special comfort found in his
Holy Word.

*I will not leave you comfortless. I will come
to you.*
John 14:18 KJV

MISSION ACCOMPLISHED

I brought glory to you here on earth by completing
the work you gave me to do.
John 17:4

It was early on a Sunday morning when the phone rang. "Hello," I answered groggily.

"Mom's gone," I heard my sister say between tears. "She died this morning."

In my eyes, the life of my mother was short-lived when she died at the tender age of 51. But in the book *The Purpose Driven Life*, Rick Warren states, "It's not our duration, but our *donation* that counts; it's not how long we live, but *how* we live that matters most to God."[2]

As I reflected on the donation my mother made during her time on earth and the legacy she left behind in her seven children, I found comfort in knowing she completed the work God gave her to do.

Jesus spent 33 years on earth fulfilling the mission God gave Him to do. And when He died on the cross at the tender age of 33, He could say with confidence that He had fulfilled the mission His Father gave Him to do.

What is the milestone you have completed as you live your midlife years? Did you recently retire from a long and illustrious career? Did you launch your children out of your nest, and they are living life successfully on their own? Were you the primary caregiver of your mother or father until God called them home? Although your time has ended regarding the milestone you completed, may you find comfort in knowing you gave it your all and completed the work God gave you to do.

"Well done, good and faithful servant. Well done."

PRAY

Father, may I find comfort as I live my midlife years knowing I accomplished the mission You gave me to do. Amen.

DIGGING DEEPER

What is one milestone you are completing as you live your midlife years? Although it is ending, how are you comforted knowing you gave it your all?

Well done, my good and faithful servant. You have been faithful in handling this small amount, so now I will give you many more responsibilities.
Matthew 25:21

A SAFE PLACE

The name of the Lord is a strong fortress;
the godly run to him and are safe.
Proverbs 18:10

Bang! Bang! Bang! The shots awakened us abruptly out of our sleep. We looked out the window to see what was happening. After seeing nothing unusual, we surmised that someone was shooting at another wild animal invading our neighborhood, so my husband and I returned soundly to sleep.

We slept until we were awakened the next morning by a knock on our door from the police, questioning us about a murder that had occurred overnight.

There was a time in our world when you could move to a safer neighborhood or city to get away from the violence occurring in the world. But today, no matter where you live, no place is safe anymore. According to a report published by Statista Research Department, on July 5, 2021, there were roughly 1.2 million violent crimes committed in 2019 in the United States. This number can be compared to the total number of property crimes, roughly 6.93 million that year. Of violent crimes in 2019, there were 821,182 aggravated assaults, making this offense the most common of violent crime offenses.[3]

Based on these statistics, is there any place where you can feel safe in an unsafe world as you live your midlife years? According to Proverbs 18:10, the righteous can take refuge in the name of the Lord as a strong tower because it signifies the attributes by which he is known—attributes of mercy, grace, longsuffering, goodness, and truth. This strong tower will not only serve as a source of safety when a crime occurs but also as a source of comfort and peace when we are affected by it.

When it seems there is no place to run for safety anymore as you live your midlife years, never forget there is one place to go. Run to the safe place found in the arms of the Lord, the place where He can keep you from becoming alarmed.

PRAY

Father, thank You for being a source of safety I can run to as I live my midlife years. Amen.

DIGGING DEEPER

How does knowing God is a refuge you can run to during your time of trouble provide you with a source of comfort as you live your midlife years?

This I declare about the Lord: He alone is my refuge, my place of safety, he is my God, and I trust him.
Psalms 91:2

LIVING BETWEEN THE DASH

Teach us to number our days and recognize how few they are; help us spend them as we should.
Psalms 90:12 TLB

She was only fifty-eight, yet I stood over her, wondering how a once physically robust and energetic woman laid lifeless before me in a casket, after losing her battle with brain cancer.

But although my friend died at what I considered an untimely age, it was obvious by the large attendance at her funeral and the words of love and admiration expressed by family, friends, and colleagues that for her short life, she lived her dash.

What is the dash? The dash on our tombstone represents the years we live between our birth and our death. According to Kerry Shook in his book, *One Month to Live*, "Each person's life comes down to what transpired between those two dates. Are we living between the dash, knowing fully who we are and why we're here? Or dashing to live, hurriedly spending precious time chasing things that don't matter?"[4]

The death of a loved one or dear friend offers us an opportunity to stop and evaluate if we are living our lives as we should during our midlife years. Are we living according to God's plan and purpose for our lives? Are we taking care of our minds, spirits, and bodies? Are we taking time to nurture our relationship with Christ and spending time reading God's Word? Or are we, as Mr. Shook asks, simply dashing to live, hurriedly spending precious time doing those things that in the end will not matter?

As I said my final goodbye to my friend and listened to others speak about her life, I found comfort in knowing she lived her years well between her dash until God called her home. What about you? In the words of poet Linda Ellis from her poem, "The Dash":

"When your eulogy is being read, with your life's actions to rehash, will others find comfort in how you lived your dash during your midlife years?"[5]

PRAY

Father, when I'm no longer on this
earth, may others find great comfort
in how I sought to live my life for
You during my midlife years. Amen.

DIGGING DEEPER

Spend some time evaluating your life.
In what ways do you need to
improve your "dash" as you live your
midlife years?

*Your life is like the morning fog—it's here
a little while, then it's gone.*
James 4:14

WHEN YOU

FEEL LIKE A
FAILURE

WHEN THE ROOSTER CROWS

If we confess our sins, he is faithful and just
and will forgive us our sins and purify us
from all unrighteousness.
I John 1:9 NIV

When money became tight as I prepared for my career as a Christian author, I interviewed for several full-time jobs that I felt qualified to do. But each time I applied, the reply was the same: "Thank you for applying but we hired another candidate." Like the rooster who crowed every morning in my neighbor's yard, each letter or email received with the same reply was a steady reminder of my failed attempts to find a job to help meet my financial needs.

Peter may have also felt like a failure each time the rooster crowed after he denied Jesus three times. The good news is Jesus did not leave Peter wallowing in his failure. He told Peter he would pray that his faith would not fail (Luke 22:32).

In what ways is the rooster of failure crowing in your life as you live your midlife years? Did you have an affair that led to the end of your marriage? Did you abuse your health and you're now living with a debilitating disease? Did you lose your temper at work and you're now looking for another job when you were close to retiring from the one you had? When the rooster of failure crows loudly in your ear because of mistakes you have made, remember that Jesus is always praying for you as He prayed for Peter—praying that your faith will not fail. We serve a God who forgives and who can restore you to living the life He created for you to live.

Need proof? Just ask Peter.

PRAY

Father, when I hear the rooster of failure crowing in my ear because of my mistakes, remind me You are a God who will help me recover from them all. Amen.

DIGGING DEEPER

In what ways do you need to accept God's offer of forgiveness as you live your midlife years so the rooster of failure can stop crowing in your life?

Restore to me the joy of your salvation and make me willing to obey you.
Psalms 51:12

CHANGING YOUR TRAJECTORY

This is the confidence we have in approaching God: that if we ask anything according to his will, he hears us.

I John 5:14 NIV

Did you know that in biblical times a name meant everything? For a young man named Jabez, his name meant that he would grow up to live a life filled with pain; yet when Jabez prayed and asked God to change the destiny of his life, God granted his request.

Now this doesn't mean we can ask God for anything and get a yes from Him every time. It does mean that if we ask anything according to His perfect will for our lives, He hears us.

For example, Jabez asked God to bless him, and He did. He asked God to keep him from harm and pain, and God did. In short, because Jabez asked for a life filled with blessings and not pain, God not only heard his prayer but granted his request.

Maybe you've made some attempts at trying to achieve some great things in your life and you've failed. The launch of a business, the start of a relationship that failed, or a risky investment in the stock market failed. Henry Ford has aptly said, "Failure is not an opportunity to give up but simply an opportunity to begin again, this time more intelligently."

What would you still like to accomplish as you live your midlife years? Do you want to attend college to finish your degree, launch your dream business, or travel to a remote land? No matter what has previously happened in your life that has caused you pain, don't allow the failures of your past to prevent you from moving forward. If you want to change the trajectory of your life as you live your midlife years from one of pain to one filled with blessings, ask God for His help to live the life you desire. Then stand back and watch as He grants your request.

PRAY

Father, please change the trajectory
of my life from one of failure to
success as I live my midlife years.
Amen.

DIGGING DEEPER

What is one area of your life that
you'd like to change from failure to
success as you live your midlife
years? How will you depend upon
the Word of God to help you
accomplish your goal?

*May he grant your heart's desires and
make all your plans succeed.*
Psalms 20:4

COMMIT IT TO HIM

Commit everything you do to the Lord.
Trust him, and he will help you.
Psalms 37:5

I participate in a morning exercise program twice a week with an older group of women. Because I can join them during the morning hours, the inevitable question arises: "Are you retired?"

My reply is always, "No."

But I am not the only one. According to the Association of Long-Term Care Planning (www.altcp.org), despite being better planners, many midlife women still end up feeling they're not ready for retirement, and 40 percent of women revealed they don't have enough money saved for retirement.[6]

How is this possible?

The reasons are varied. You had to withdraw money from your retirement account to pay off debt or to fund your child's college tuition. You took the money out to take care of a major medical bill or to place a parent in a nursing facility. Or you may have been a frivolous spender and never set aside money for your retirement.

King David tells us in the book of Psalms to "commit everything [we] do to the Lord; trust him to help [us] do it and he will" (Psalms 37:5 TLB). This means not only entrusting our lives, our families, our jobs, and our possessions to God but also our retirement years. Despite what your retirement account looks like as you live your midlife years, commit what you have set aside for your retirement to the Lord, and then trust Him to take care of you better than any retirement plan ever could.

PRAY

Father, I commit my retirement years
to You because I know You can take
care of me better than my retirement
plan ever could. Amen.

DIGGING DEEPER

Are your retirement years fast
approaching as you live your midlife
years? In what ways do you need to
commit them to God?

Commit your actions to the Lord and
your plans will succeed.
Proverbs 16:3

RECOVERING FROM OUR FALLS

For though the righteous fall seven times,
they rise again, but the wicked stumble
when calamity strikes.
Proverbs 24:16(a)

One day during my morning walk, I had a nasty fall. I was stiff and sore the next day but grateful that although I took a hard fall, I got back up again.

Like my nasty fall, life has a way of causing us to fall hard at times as we live our midlife years. The ending of a long-standing marriage or a long-term relationship that we thought would lead to marriage. The loss of a job after working for the same company for several years. Finding out we have a life-threatening illness after visiting our doctor for a routine checkup. Midlife challenges that may knock us down so hard that we may wonder if we will ever recover from our tumultuous fall and get back up again.

But no matter how hard the falls that occur in our lives as we live our midlife years, we can find comfort in knowing there is someone who not only experienced a bad fall in his life but got back up again. For Jesus Christ was beaten, crucified, and placed in a borrowed tomb after He died on a cross, but He did not remain there. On the third day, according to the scriptures, He recovered from His tumultuous fall when He arose from the grave with all authority and power in His hands (Matthew 28:5, 6, 18, NLT).

The same power that can help you recover from your falls and get back up again.

PRAYER

Father, thank You for rising from the dead with all power and authority to help me rise above any problem I face today. Amen.

DIGGING DEEPER

In what way have you fallen hard as you live your midlife years? How will your faith in God help you to get back up again?

The godly may trip seven times, but they will get up again. But one disaster is enough to overthrow the wicked.
Proverbs 24:16

WHEN YOU

NEED TO
FORGIVE

GO AND BE RECONCILED

So if you are presenting a sacrifice at the altar in the Temple and you suddenly remember that someone has something against you, leave your sacrifice there at the altar. Go and be reconciled to that person. Then come and offer your sacrifice to God.
Matthew 5:23-24

For years, we lived life together. Attended the same church together. Got married together. Birthed and raised children together. Laughed and cried together. Yet, when I accidentally gave away the surprise birthday party of one of the ladies in my life group, I was hurt when no one believed it was an innocent mistake. As my anger simmered, I realized for our relationship to continue, forgiveness was necessary, not only from these women for my mistake, but also from me.

Jesus understood the importance of restoring broken relationships. He shared in the Sermon on the Mount that before a person offered a sacrifice to his Father in the temple, they had to first seek forgiveness from their fellow man for any wrongs they had done towards them. Once they sought forgiveness from the person they offended and reconciled their broken relationship, they could bring their offering to the altar.

Jesus' instructions are equally relevant when we find ourselves in the position of needing to forgive someone who has wronged us. A spouse who revealed their love for you has gone cold and filed for divorce. A child who denounced their belief in God and is living a lifestyle different from the values you instilled in them. A friend who betrayed your confidence after secrets shared in private were shared in public.

Restoring broken relationships is paramount to your heavenly Father as you live your midlife years. So whether someone needs to forgive you for a wrong you've done to them, or you need to forgive someone for a wrong they've done to you, leave your sacrifice at the altar and go and be reconciled.

PRAY

Father, give me a desire as I live my midlife years to go, forgive, and be reconciled. Amen.

DIGGING DEEPER

Is there a broken relationship in your life that needs restoration as you live your midlife years? What can you do today to be the first to restore it?

Love prospers when a fault is forgiven, but dwelling on it separates close friends.
Proverbs 17:9

WERE IT NOT FOR GRACE

Each time I received the news about one of my girlfriend's divorces during my midlife years, I made every effort to avoid crossing paths with their ex-husband. If I did encounter him, the only words I felt might escape from my lips were not, "Hello, how are you?" but rather, "Hello, I don't like you anymore."

After sharing my sentiments one day with an older woman I highly respected, she shared these poignant words: "Be careful how you treat your friends' husbands after their divorce. If it weren't for the grace of God, you could be in their shoes. "

She was right. Statistics indicate one in five couples will get divorced, and divorces among women in midlife are on the rise.[7] Yet, despite my marital struggles, God has allowed my marriage to survive. It has weathered financial challenges, my insecurities as a breast cancer survivor, and even those moments when I gave my husband the cold shoulder over trivial matters.

It was the grace of God that prevented my marriage from becoming a statistic. And when extending grace becomes difficult, those are the moments when I must look to the One who continually extends grace to me.

When life's twists and turns lead you to unexpected places as you live your midlife years and extending grace becomes difficult to do, keep looking to the One - the One who extends grace to you.

PRAY

Father, help me to extend the same grace to others who I feel don't deserve it that You extend me every day as I live my midlife years.

DIGGING DEEPER

Who do you need to extend God's grace to as you live your midlife years that deserves it the least?

God saved you by his grace when you believed. And you can't take credit for this; it is a gift from God.
Ephesians 2:8

THE GOD OF SECOND CHANCES

During my young adult years, my father almost died after suffering a heart attack. But through the hands of a skillful surgeon placing tiny stents inside my father's heart to replace his clogged arteries, my father received a second chance at life. A second chance to rebuild and restore a relationship between him and me that I felt was over long ago.

But my dad never gave up. With dogged determination and a deep love for me, he kept chiseling away at the wall of bitterness I had formed between us until one day that wall came crashing down.

My father is no longer with me as I live my midlife years. As I reflect on the wonderful memories we created together after our relationship was restored, I am so thankful for the time we had together. I am thankful I gave him a second chance.

Whether it is a parent, friend, child, or boss, forgiveness is never easy, especially when the wrong committed to you has been great. Forgiveness is a necessary part of the fruit Jesus expects us to produce as we live our midlife years. When you find it hard to forgive those who have wronged you, remember to look to the One who forgives you greatly. To the one always willing to give you a second chance.

PRAY

Father, thank You for being a God
always willing to give me a second
chance as I live my midlife years.
Amen.

DIGGING DEEPER

In what ways are you still harboring
unforgiveness towards someone as
you live your midlife years? What
step can you take today to give that
person a second chance?

*Jesus answered, "I tell you, not seven times,
but seventy-seven times.
Matthew 18:22 NIV*

COMBATING THE INVADER WITHIN

My retirement years are fast approaching. Each time I've attended the party of a friend or colleague who has retired, I felt the invader of guilt rising within because I am not as prepared for my approaching retirement years as I wanted to be.

Although external enemies were a constant threat to the city of Jerusalem—and guards patrolled day and night against their threats—inside the city, murder, robbery, violence, and wickedness were rampant. While King David sought to protect his beloved city from outside invaders, he began to realize protection was also needed from the invaders within.

As we live our midlife years, we too need to watch out for internal invaders. The guilt of our failures as wives, mothers, professionals, and friends has a way of rising periodically within our minds and hearts. We're relentlessly reminded of what we've done or have not done. Guilt makes us feel not only unworthy of forgiveness from others but also unworthy of forgiveness from ourselves.

How can we combat the invader of guilt that rises periodically from within? While we cannot erase the mistakes we have made as we live our midlife years, we can be kind to ourselves and forgive ourselves in the same way Jesus encouraged us to be kind and treat others.

Why is forgiving yourself for your mistakes so important? Research has shown that forgiving yourself can reap huge rewards for your health as you live your midlife years. Rewards that include lowering the risk of a heart attack, lowering your blood pressure, improving your sleep, and reducing your levels of anxiety, depression, and stress.[8]

Based on these benefits, will you choose to forgive yourself today for the mistakes you have made as you live your midlife years? In the words of Dr. Karen Swartz, Director of the Mood Disorders Adult Consultation Clinic at The Johns Hopkins Hospital: "Forgiveness is a choice. You are choosing to offer compassion and empathy to the person who wronged you.[9]

And sometimes the person who needs forgiveness the most is you.

PRAY

Father, when the invader of guilt
attacks my heart as I live my midlife
years, help me to combat it by
remembering to forgive myself as
You forgive me. Amen.

DIGGING DEEPER

In what ways do you need to forgive
yourself so you can reap the mental,
physical, and spiritual rewards self-
forgiveness offers your health as you
live your midlife years?

*Kind words are like honey—
sweet to the soul and healthy for the body.*
Proverbs 16:24

WHEN YOU

NEED
GUIDANCE

WALK THIS WAY

While watching a speckle-colored orange robin looking for worms in my backyard one morning, I noticed he stopped in one spot, put his head into the ground, but didn't find any worms. Then he stopped in another spot, put his little head down again, and still didn't find any worms. Then suddenly, as if he heard someone say, "Go there," he walked his little legs over to another spot, placed his head in the ground, and up came a worm.

I could not help but think how our heavenly Father does the same for us. When our lives have us going in various directions to find solutions to the various problems we encounter as we live our midlife years, sometimes we just need to be still until He tells us what to do. Is it time to kick a young adult child out of your home who doesn't want to abide by your rules? Should you keep trying to make your marriage work? Is it time to retire when you're making mistakes on your job that you've never made before?

When you need guidance about the best path to take regarding a difficult decision you must make as you live your midlife years, trust the wisdom and advice your heavenly Father gives. As you listen to His voice advising you on what to do, you can be sure He will never lead you the wrong way.

PRAY

Father, thank You for the guidance I receive from You as I live my midlife years. As I follow Your advice for my life, I know You will never lead me the wrong way. Amen.

DIGGING DEEPER

Are you at a crossroads regarding a difficult decision you need to make as you live your midlife years? What is God telling you through his Holy Word about which path to take?

The steps of a good man are ordered by the Lord, and He delights in his way.
Psalms 37:23 NKJV

FOLLOWING THE RULE OF PEACE

And let the peace that comes from Christ
rule in your heart.
Colossians 3:15

Oftentimes, when we needed additional monies to make ends meet, I was torn internally between whether to return to work or remain home to keep pursuing my dream to become a professional writer. And what helped me decide is when I followed the rule of peace.

The word rule, according to one Bible dictionary, comes from the language of athletics. An umpire is responsible for administering the rules of an athletic game to determine whether a player is playing fairly or unfairly. The apostle Paul acts as our umpire administering the rules of living this Christian life. In his letter to the Colossians, Paul explains that we must allow the peace that comes from knowing Christ to be the ruler of our hearts when we experience internal conflict about a difficult decision we need to make as we live our midlife years.

Should I have the risky surgery my doctor is recommending, or take my chances with my health as is? Is it time to put my parents in a nursing home, or do I continue taking care of them on my own? Do I take a chance on marriage after living as a single woman for years?

When you're facing a decision that is causing much internal conflict as you live your midlife years, remember to follow the choice that gives you the most peace—the choice that comes from knowing the Ruler of peace.

PRAY

Father, may every decision I make as
I live my midlife years give me the
peace that only You can provide.
Amen.

DIGGING DEEPER

What is a difficult decision you need
to make today as you live your
midlife years? How will you use the
rule of peace to help you make the
right choice?

*You will keep in perfect peace all who trust
in you,
all whose thoughts are fixed on you!
Isaiah 26:3*

ARE YOU LOST WITHOUT IT?

Your word is a lamp to guide my feet and
a light for my path.
Psalms 119:105

During my vacation travels with my family through the years, I visited several hotels and always found it comforting when I opened the nightstand drawer and found a Bible stationed within. But one time while traveling, after a long day of sightseeing, I opened the nightstand to read the Bible and to my surprise, it wasn't there.

I thought, *What would I do if I could not have access to God's Word anymore?*

Why is having access to God's word so important as we live our midlife years? The book of II Timothy shares several benefits:

- It convicts us when we sin.

- It corrects us when we do wrong.

- It places our footsteps on the right path.

- It equips us to live life effectively.

The writer of Psalms 119 understood the importance of having access to the Word of God. He loved the word so much that the Bible records how he meditated on it whenever he got a chance—morning, noon, and night. Having access to God's Word seemed as important to him as having access to food or water.

Is that your desire as well as you live your midlife years?

Continue to hide the Word in your heart. That's the one safe place no one can ever take it away.

PRAY

Father, I promise to hide Your Word
deep within my heart as I live my
midlife years to ensure no one ever
takes Your Word away from me.
Amen.

DIGGING DEEPER

How are you hiding God's Word in
your heart as you live your midlife
years to ensure it can never be taken
from you?

*Oh, how I love your law! I meditate on it
all day long.*
Psalms 119:97 NIV

FATHER KNOWS BEST

Show me the right path, O Lord. Point out
the road for me to follow.
Psalms 25:4

I enjoyed giving my children advice when they were young and came to me about a difficult decision they needed to make. But when the decision was of such magnitude that I felt like my advice was not sufficient, I told them to talk to their dad.

As King of Israel, David was tasked with the responsibility of making several difficult decisions and was surrounded by advisors who offered him advice on what to do. But he understood their counsel wasn't always enough; sometimes the decision was of such magnitude that he had to seek greater advice, advice he could only get from above.

Are you facing a major decision as you live your midlife years and are feeling unsure about what to do? Unsure of which road to follow? Unsure of which path to take? Those are the times to consult with your heavenly Father. The one who promises to listen to your concerns and provide you with sound and wise advice. The one who promises never to lead you the wrong way.

Is it time for you to talk to your heavenly Father?

PRAY

Father, thank You for being my
heavenly Father; the one I can always
go to when I need guidance and
direction as I live my midlife years.
Amen.

DIGGING DEEPER

What is a major problem you will
seek your heavenly Father's advice
and direction for today?

*Your word is a lamp to guide my
feet and a light for my path.
Psalms 119:105*

WHEN YOU'RE

UNDER
PRESSURE

BUILT TO WITHSTAND

Anyone who listens to my teaching and follows it is wise, like a person who builds a house on solid rock.
Matthew 7:24

In a beachside neighborhood in the city of Mexico Beach, Florida, it still stands. A two-story, four-bedroom, four-and-a-half bath, white-framed house remained amongst the rubble of other homes around it after Hurricane Michael pummeled the town and sought to destroy everything in its path.

How did this one house survive the wrath of the wicked storm? It still stands because it was built to withstand.

While teaching to the masses as part of His Sermon on the Mount, Jesus said that those who listen to His teachings and obey them in every arena of their lives are like a builder who lays a solid foundation for his house. When life's storms arise that seek to destroy us, we won't collapse if we are standing on the firm foundation we have laid through our relationship with Jesus Christ, and because of the promises He has given in His Word to take care of us during our life's storms.

You've fallen behind on your property taxes and just received notice that your home is about to be foreclosed; you're not getting interviews for jobs you're qualified to do and wonder if it's because you are being discriminated against because of your age. Your child announces they no longer identify with their gender and want to be called by a different name.

How can you keep standing through it all?

Because you were built to withstand.

PRAY

Father, thank You for the firm foundation I have laid for my life in knowing Your son, the one who helps me keep standing through every storm I encounter as I live my midlife years. Amen.

DIGGING DEEPER

How will the foundation of faith you have built in Jesus Christ help to sustain you through the life storms you encounter as you live your midlife years?

For no one can lay any foundation other than the one we already have—Jesus Christ.
I Corinthians 3:11

DON'T STOP LIVING

Build homes, and plan to stay. Plant
gardens and eat the food they
produce. Marry and have children. Then
find spouses for them so that you may have
many grandchildren. Multiply! Do not
dwindle away!
Jeremiah 29:5-6

Ever since I left my career in higher education to pursue a career as a professional writer, I've struggled financially. And I've often wondered as I've focused on doing the work of writing through the years how long it would be before I'd see the light at the end of my long tunnel. But despite not knowing if I would ever attain financial success in my life as a Christian author, I continued with the business of writing.

While in slavery to the Babylonians, the Israelites asked God how long they would remain in captivity. Through the prophet Jeremiah, he instructed them to "build homes, plant gardens, marry and have children" (Jeremiah 29:5-6). They were not to allow their lives to halt just because they were in captivity.

Sometimes the problems we encounter as we live our midlife years will cause us to place a brake on moving forward with other aspects of our lives. You became the unexpected caregiver of your parents or a grandchild. Your young adult child and his family have returned to live with you. You have put the brakes on living a life of leisure and retirement. You're wondering how long it will be before you see a light at the end of your long tunnel and live the life you planned to live.

Whether it's a physical, financial, or family challenge you've been enduring for a while as you live your midlife years, don't give up on the business of living. Keep doing what God has purposed you to do until deliverance comes.

PRAY

Father, life is not going quite the way
I planned it right now as I live my
midlife years but help me not to give
up on the business of living. Amen.

DIGGING DEEPER

In what small way, with the help of
your faith in God, can you start living
again amid an ongoing problem or
situation occurring in your life as you
live your midlife years?

*So let's not get tired of doing what is good.
At just the right time we will reap a harvest
of blessing if we don't give up.
Galatians 6:9*

CHARACTER IN THE DARK

These trials are only to test your faith to
show
that it is strong and pure.
I Peter 1:7 TLB

After a long and valiant fight with his health, we laid my brother-in-law to rest. As his friends and family members shared their tributes, I kept hearing that despite his health problems, he never complained. Actually, he encouraged others when they came to encourage him. That spoke volumes to me about his character.

What is character? Character is how we act not in the light, but in the dark. It is how we act when we find ourselves in the darkness of health problems, job problems, marital problems, financial problems, or family problems.

For example, Job demonstrated great character while in the dark after losing everything. Rather than disowning God as his wife encouraged him to do, he said, "Naked I came from my mother's womb, and naked I will depart. The Lord gave and the Lord has taken away; may the name of the Lord be praised" (Job 1:21 NIV).

Jesus also demonstrated great character while in the dark. When He hung dying on a cross, rather than asking a legion of angels to come and deliver Him to prove to others He was the Savior of the world, He shared these words, "Father, I entrust My spirit into Your hands!" (Luke 23:46).

A quote in the *New Life Application Bible* states: "We can't know the depth of our character until we see how we react under pressure."[10]

Your health is failing, your spouse has asked for a divorce, and you have become the primary caregiver of your elderly parent. When the pressures that come with living life during your midlife years test every ounce of faith you have, may it be said you were as faithful in the dark as you are in the light.

PRAY

Father, it's dark right now as I live
my midlife years but while I am here,
may You find me still faithful. Amen.

DIGGING DEEPER

What personal challenge are you
facing today that is testing the depth
of your faith in God? How will you
continue to trust God while in the
dark?

*For you know that when your faith is
tested, your endurance has a chance to grow.*
James 1:3

A PRESCRIPTION FOR YOUR SOUL

*"I will give you back your health and heal
your wounds," says the Lord.*
Jeremiah 30:17

I will be the first to admit that when I am feeling ill and my doctor gives me a prescription, I don't always follow the doctor's orders, because I dislike taking medicine. Yet I also know if I don't take the medicine, I won't get any better.

Did you know the same principle applies to God's Word? When the cares of our lives have us feeling ill, God has written a prescription we can follow in the form of His Word to help us feel better. But like the prescription my doctor gives me, it won't work if we don't follow it. If we don't open and take our daily dose of the medicine He's given to help us heal, we won't get better.

Unmet life goals. Unexpected weight gains due to hormonal changes. Children returning to the nest. Learning how to reinvent yourself after your children are gone. Are any of these issues causing you to feel stressed out as you live your midlife years? Take a dose of the prescription—the Word of God—given by the Master Doctor, the only medicine guaranteed to bring relief to your weary soul.

PRAY

Father, thank You for the healing medicine found in Your Holy Word. May I use it to receive the relief I need. Amen.

DIGGING DEEPER

Make a list of scripture verses you plan to use to provide spiritual relief from a trial currently occurring in your life as you live your midlife years.

Give all your worries and cares to God, for he cares about you.
I Peter 5:7

WHEN YOUR

FAITH NEEDS
REFRESHING

HE HASN'T MOVED

Come close to God, and God will come close
to you.
James 4:8(a)

In my 33 years of marriage, there have been times when I have not felt as close to my husband as I did when we first married. During those times, I realized it was not because he still did not desire to be close to me; I just had to do whatever it took to draw close to him again.

The same rule applies to our relationship with our heavenly Father. When we feel distant from the Lord, it's not because He has waned in His desire to be close to us; rather, it may be that we've allowed our relationship with Him through the years to become distant for one reason or the other. We're not spending as much time reading the Bible as we used to. Our prayer life has become haphazard. We've become slack in attending church regularly and fellowshipping with like-minded believers. How can we draw close to God again during those times in our lives when we feel so far away? Here are five ways shared in the book of James 4:7-10:

- Humble yourself: Admit your dependence on God to live the Christian life.

- Yield to God's authority: Submit to His will and authority for your life.

- Resist the devil's attack: Be mindful that he is trying to destroy your relationship with God.

- Purify your heart: Determine to live a life that honors God in all you do.

- Confess your sins: Admit any unconfessed sin in your life.

Like a good husband, God still desires to be close to you. During those moments when you're feeling distant from Him as you live your midlife years, spend some time renewing your relationship with Him using the five strategies listed above, and you'll find He's been there all along.

PRAY

Father, I'm ready to do whatever it takes to be close to You again as I live my midlife years. Amen.

DIGGING DEEPER

Which of the strategies do you need to use to draw close to your heavenly Father again as you live your midlife years?

But as for me, how good it is to be near God. I have made the Sovereign Lord my shelter, and I will tell everyone about the wonderful things you do.
Psalms 73:28

ARE YOU ABIDING?

I am the vine, you are the branches. Those
who remain in me and I in them will
produce much fruit, for apart from me, you
can do nothing.
John 15:5

Lately, I've missed my quiet time with the Lord. On some mornings, I've awakened late and missed my quiet time, whereas on other mornings, I've awoken on time, but allowed distractions to interfere with my time with the Lord.

Could it be that's why I haven't written as consistently as I should? Although I've set a goal to write every day, has my writing been sporadic because my time with the Lord has been sporadic?

Jesus used the illustration of the vine and branch to remind us that we must remain connected to Him if we are to be effective in our lives as believers. As we seek to maintain a regular relationship with Him through prayer, worship, and Bible study, He states there will be a direct correlation in the "fruit" we produce.

If you have been struggling lately with your quality time with the Lord as you live your midlife years, confess your struggle. Then recommit to developing your relationship again with Him. For apart from the "vine," you can do nothing. Attached to it, you can do everything!

PRAY

Father, forgive me for my
inconsistency in spending quality
time with You.
I recommit to spending time with
You once again so I can
produce much fruit for You as I live
my midlife years. Amen.

DIGGING DEEPER

How can you improve your quality
time with God so you are producing
the "fruit" He wants to produce
through you as you live your midlife
years?

I appointed you to go and produce lasting
fruit, so that the Father will give you
whatever you ask for, using my name.
John 15:16(b)

RECLAIMING YOUR SABBATH

You have six days each week for your
ordinary work but the seventh day is a
Sabbath day of rest dedicated to
the Lord your God.
Exodus 20:9-10

I contacted my hairdresser to see if I could get in for a much-needed appointment. She replied, "Friday and Saturday are busy this week. How about Sunday?"

Sunday? But isn't Sunday the day I am supposed to rest and refresh?

As the Israelites prepared to enter the Promised Land, God told them to set aside one day of the week to worship and rest. He commanded it because He knew the Israelites needed a day of unhurried time for worship, relaxation, and rest.

Keeping the Sabbath today is not a requirement because we are free from the Old Testament law (Colossians 2:14-17). Although God does not require us to set aside one day of the week to worship and rest, someone has aptly said, "To observe a regular time of rest and worship in our fast-paced world shows how important God is to us, and it gives us the extra benefit of refreshing our spirits."

In his article, "The Lost Practice of Resting One Day Each Week", Joshua Becker shares six benefits of concentrated rest for our mind, body, and soul: a healthier body, less stress, deeper relationships, an opportunity for reflection, balance, and increased production.[11]

It's no coincidence that these are some of the same benefits we desire as we live our midlife years. These are benefits designed to help us live our lives effectively for ourselves, our God, and others.

If you have lost the practice of resting one day a week because of the many obligations on your plate, rededicate your Sabbath day to the Lord. You'll find the benefits of worship, rest, and refreshment totally worth it when Monday comes.

PRAY

Father, thank You for Your commandment to set aside one day a week to worship and rest. I recommit today to honoring Your command to rest and refresh as I live my midlife years. Amen.

DIGGING DEEPER

What adjustments do you need to make to reclaim your Sabbath day in your life as you live your midlife years?

Come to me, all you who are weary and burdened, and I will give you rest.
Matthew 11:28

IS IT TIME FOR A WALK?

Physical training is good, but training for
godliness is much better, promising benefits
in this life and in the life to come.
I Timothy 4:8

Every so often when I need re-energizing, I take a long, brisk walk. I know that walking provides many benefits to my physical as well as my mental health. These benefits include improving my cardiovascular health, burning calories, boosting my energy, and improving my mood.

Oftentimes, when I am weary from the cares of my life and my faith needs re-energizing, I like to take another long walk. I walk down the Hall of Faith found in Hebrews, chapter 11.

On my Hebrews 11 walk, I am spiritually refreshed when I look around and see the many people who lived a life of great faith. I see Noah who built an ark by faith when it had never rained a day in his life. I see Abraham who believed by faith that God would produce a nation through him if he left his homeland and moved to a totally new place. I see Sarai who believed by faith that she would have a child, even though she was old and barren.

I Timothy 4:8 states: "Physical training is good, but training for godliness is much better, promising benefits in this life and in the life to come."

Take advantage of the benefits of taking a good, brisk walk for your physical health as you live your midlife years. And when problems arise and your faith needs a boost of energy to keep going, take a good brisk walk down the hall of faith.

PRAY

Father, thank You for the Hall of
Faith which inspires me to keep
walking. Amen.

DIGGING DEEPER

Which person or persons inspire you
in the Hall of Faith to keep walking
by faith as you live your midlife
years? Why?

For we walk by faith, not by sight.
II Corinthians 5:7 NKJV

WHEN YOU
WORRY

UP, UP, AND AWAY

When she was younger, my daughter participated in an event at our church in which the youth were told to write their worries on a flat balloon. After inflating the balloon, they went outside and released their balloons into the air until they disappeared.

This is a wonderful illustration of what the apostle Peter meant when he told the first century Christians to release their worries and cares to the Lord. It did not mean their problems would disappear into thin air like the balloons, but as they released their worries and cares about their lives to the God who cared for them, He would replace their worries with a peace far beyond their understanding.

What is causing you so much angst as you live your midlife years? Is it a young adult child who has decided to follow another religion or none? Is it a marriage that has lost its fire? Maybe you wonder whether you will ever be able to retire or keep working until you die.

As you live your midlife years, are the ill effects of worry causing your health to deteriorate, disrupting your productivity at work, or affecting your relationships with your family and/or friends? Take a moment to release your worries, one by one, to the One who cares for you.

PRAY

Father, when I worry about the cares of my life as I live my midlife years, help me to release every worry into Your loving hands. Amen.

DIGGING DEEPER

What is one worry you need to release to God as you live your midlife years?

Give your burdens to the Lord and he will take care of you.
He will not permit the godly to slip and fall.
Psalms 55:22

JUST ENOUGH FAITH

When she was in elementary school, my daughter wanted to attend an after-school program her school offered, but I told her we couldn't afford it. Without hesitation, she said, "Mom, I know how we can afford my after-school program."

"How, babe?"

"By publishing your book. When you publish your book, you'll have lots of money!"

My daughter was small, but big in faith. She reminded me of the mustard seed Jesus described in the Sermon on the Mount. He shared that just like the mustard seed produces a great plant once buried, it only takes a small amount of faith, once planted, to move the mountains that arise in our lives. Whether it be a mountain of debt, a mountain of health problems, or a mountain of work piled high upon our office desk, He wants us to believe that with just a little bit of faith in Him, nothing we seek to accomplish will be impossible.

My daughter's belief in me that I would one day publish was just enough to activate my faith and ask God for the means to enroll my daughter in her after-school program. Not only did He provide the monetary resources for her to attend the first year, but she was able to attend each year thereafter until she completed elementary school.

Does the faith you have in God seem small in comparison to the mountain you face in your life as you live your midlife years? Give Him the small amount of faith you have just like my daughter chose to do, and you may find it's just enough for God to work with to do the impossible.

PRAY

Father, my faith seems small to me today, but I'm grateful for the reminder that it's just enough, with Your help, to move any mountain I face as I live my midlife years. Amen.

DIGGING DEEPER

In what ways can you activate the faith that seems small to you to combat the mountains you face today as you live your midlife years?

"What do you mean, 'If I can'?" Jesus asked. "Anything is possible if a person believes."
Mark 9:23

LOOK AT THE BIRDS

Look at the birds of the air; they do not sow or reap or store away in barns, and yet your heavenly Father feeds them. Are you not much more valuable than they?
Matthew 6:26

I confess. I worry. As I live on one income, fleshing out the call of writing God called me to do, I worry about how I will pay all the bills sitting on my desk. I worry about how I will take care of the much-needed repairs around my home. I worry about my approaching retirement years.

Then I'm reminded to look at the birds. They don't worry. They just soar through the air doing exactly what they have been created to do.

What are you worrying about as you live your midlife years? Are you worried about the health of your mom or dad? Do you wonder about whether you'll survive menopause? Do you ask whether you'll be able to send your child to college because the cost of tuition has skyrocketed? Do you worry if you'll be one of the employees laid off because your company is downsizing?

Whatever the worry, God does not want it to consume you. Instead, He wants you to focus on living out the mission He has given you during your midlife years whether that is living life as a mother, wife, caregiver, or professional. Keep living your life with purpose. When you find yourself worrying about your children, parents, work, health, finances, or a million other things as you live your midlife years, take a moment to look up at the birds.

PRAY

Father, when I worry about how You
will take care of me during my
midlife years, remind me to look at
how You take care of your birds.
Amen.

DIGGING DEEPER

Spend a day outside observing the
birds. Write down what you learn
from them about God's provisions
for them and you.

*That is why I tell you not to worry about
everyday life—whether you have enough food
and drink, or enough clothes to wear. Isn't
life more than food, and your body more
than clothing?*
Matthew 6:25

WHAT I KNOW FOR SURE

But you must remain faithful to the things
you have been taught. You know they are
true, for you know you can trust those who
taught you.
II Timothy 3:14

Do you remember the popular slogan used by Farmers Insurance in one of its commercials: "We know a thing or two because we've seen a thing or two"? The purpose of the commercial was to let people know they could depend on this insurance company for every insurance concern they encountered because Farmers Insurance had already covered several unusual events in the lives of their members.

The apostle Paul sought to let Timothy, his son in the ministry, know the same thing about Paul's life. As a young pastor, Timothy was discouraged about his new role, so Paul encouraged Timothy to look at Paul's life—his teachings, his purpose for living, his faith, his love, his patience, and his suffering. If Timothy could see all that God had accomplished in Paul's life as a missionary, he could draw strength from knowing God could accomplish the same thing in his life as a young pastor.

Are you feeling discouraged today? Discouraged because life is not going as you planned as you live your midlife years? Discouraged because you may be wondering if God can take care of *this* new problem occurring in your life. The sudden death of your spouse in a car accident and having to live life alone; the denial by your insurance company for a medical procedure you desperately need; a child struggling with depression and suicidal thoughts.

Take some time as you deal with the new problem that has arisen in your life to reflect on what you already know about your heavenly Father—His love and protection of you through the years, His faithfulness in never giving up on you during the many times you wanted to give up on yourself, and the promises He's already fulfilled from His holy Word to meet all your needs. Then find comfort in knowing He can take care of whatever life has brought your way today as you live your midlife years because He already has!

PRAY

Father, because You have been
faithful, may I never forget that You
will always be faithful. Amen.

DIGGING DEEPER

List five things you already know
about God's love and care for you.
How does what you already know
help you continue to trust God to
take care of you as you live your
midlife years?

*Day by day the Lord takes care of the
innocent, and they will receive an inheritance
that lasts forever.*
Psalms 37:18

ENDNOTES

He's Still Working

1. Lucado, Max, *You'll Get Through This: Hope and Help for Your Turbulent Times*, Thomas Nelson Publishers, 2015, Ch. 5, pg. 57.

Mission Accomplished

2. Warren, Rick, *The Purpose Driven Life: What on Earth Am I Here For?* Zondervan, 2002. Page 233.

A Safe Place

3. Statista Research Department, July 5, 2021

Living Between the Dash

4. Shook, Kerry and Chris, *One Month to Live - Thirty Days to a No-Regrets Life.* Waterbrook press. 2011, page 151.

5. Ellis, Linda. *The Dash, Making a Difference with Your Life,* Simple Truths; New edition. January 1, 2017

Commit It To Him

6. Stein, Samantha, *Why many women feel they're not ready for retirement.* Association for Long-Term Care Planning Blog | ALTCP.org Roundup, March 2017

Were It Not For Grace

7. Whitbourne, Susan, Ph.D., *What Rising Divorce Rates in Midlife Mean for You* Psychology Today, November 9, 2013.

Combating the Invader Within

8. Vitelli, Romeo, Ph.D. Forgiveness and your health: Can being able to forgive improve heart functioning? Forgiveness and Your Health | Psychology Today, March 2015.

9. Barth, F. Diane, L.C.S.W. Forgiving and Not Forgiving Can Both Affect Your Health | Psychology Today. January 2019

10. <u>How can the act of forgiving help my physical health? By Madison Selcho -</u> <u>Deseret News</u>, April 2023 -

Character in the Dark

11. *Life Application Study Bible, Third edition*, Tyndale House Publishers, Carol Stream, IL. Page 2167.

Reclaiming Your Sabbath

12. Becker, Joshua, *The Lost Practice of Resting One Day Each Week*. Becoming minimalist.com, April 27, 2014

Thank you for purchasing this devotional book. If you enjoyed this book, please leave a review on the author's page at Amazon.com. Also, visit the author at inspirationforliving.org to view the other inspirational books and resources she offers to inspire you on your faith journey and to join her mailing list.

Follow the author on social media at:

Facebook:
https://www.facebook.com/jeaninne.stokes

X: https://twitter.com/stokes_jeaninne

LinkedIn:
https://www.linkedin.com/in/jeaninne-stokes-607b5547/

www.ingramcontent.com/pod-product-compliance
Lightning Source LLC
Chambersburg PA
CBHW070525160726
48003CB00004B/1692